CHILD SAFEGUARDING IN SCHOOLS

DR DHEERAJ MEHROTRA

Contents

Preface

Child Safeguarding in Schools is a priority. We at schools always tend to neglect things that remain important, and hence, revisiting some of the do's and don'ts are requisite in particular.

The defined approach reflects how best we do things and contribute to the cause of quality care and concern in totality. The book Child Safeguarding In Schools is a step towards awareness to attain our wards' total safety and security and staff. A must buy for all school leaders, administrators and educators to reflect on safety as a requisite.

Dr Dheeraj Mehrotra

Author

I

Safety & Security Anchors For Schools

SAFETY & SECURITY ANCHOR

#1

School buildings need to be under surveillance on a 24×7 basis. Assure your CCTV cameras are in working order with the recording pace. A dimensional view of the recorded data should be analysed to ensure that the charges/ vice principal/ admin staff/ Principal/ Management are routine. The findings must be analysed and queried towards the students' interest in totality.

SAFETY & SECURITY ANCHOR

#2

Emergency exit plans must be in their place. Every floor must have an ENTRY and an EXIT plan on display. Check on locks and barricaders to settle the students with trained, armed guards on duty. Assure there is a public sign designating an official **meeting point** in the school. It can be called an **assembly point; ameeting point** is a fixed (safe) place where students can gather or report during an **emergency** or a fire drill etc.

SAFETY & SECURITY ANCHOR

#3

Appoint Senior Students as FLOOR in charge of managing an easy flow of the traffic class wise during recess, before and after assembly, and getting over the school. Each floor must have a TEACHER on duty and must be housed with a small staff room occupied by teachers teaching on the respective floor of the classes. Any teacher having a free period must have an eye on the students moving out for any reason.

SAFETY & SECURITY ANCHOR

#4

Preparing students to remain calm in case of attacks is how schools can ensure student safety.

This must be practised periodically through MOCK Drills. Ensure inclusive and equitable quality education and promote lifelong learning opportunities for all. The children should be given mock sessions to deal with situations like these and must not react but *contribute in a safe exit without fear and anxiety.*

SAFETY & SECURITY ANCHOR

#5

Ragging and bullying must be checked regularly. Class Monitors must be coached to inform the Head of School of any such incident in private. Teachers need to be incontrovertible partners, the front-line actors whom the students trustingly turn to for advice, guidance, and inspiration as they stand on the threshold of young adulthood. The teachers should act like extended family members to the students.

SAFETY & SECURITY ANCHOR

#6

Teachers need to govern their relationship with the students and their parents. They are monitored to be documented using the INTERACTION Register to promote safety as a PRIORITY. Parents need to submit family photographs with the child in the centre to assure liaison and networking for safety and security reasons. This record contributes to knowing the family and the child better. When teachers see signs which cause them concern, they should, as a first step, seek some clarification from the child with tact and understanding. When a classroom assistant or another member of the school's non-teaching staff sees such signs, they should immediately bring them to the class teacher's attention or the Designated Teacher. It may be appropriate for the necessary clarification to be carried out by the teacher. We also need to make sure that the parents are informed that an immediate solution may be private.

SAFETY & SECURITY ANCHOR

#7

Schools should also appoint counsellors/psychologists to help students address trauma/rage/depression issues. The objective should teach learners a set of values and a sense of moral responsibility and belong to the nation. The teacher understands the child better and can mould the child to the best format and requirements. Sound advice without AWE is a must for every student by the TEACHER.

SAFETY & SECURITY ANCHOR

#8

*Schools need to ensure that students can take care of themselves and tackle situations like abductions/ abuse. Assure the spending of money on training people and equipping them with measures of checking CHILD ABUSE/ **POCSO** or The Protection of Children from Sexual Offences **Act** (**POCSO Act**). School management must ensure at least two workshops on CHILD ABUSE in every session.*

SAFETY & SECURITY ANCHOR

#9

Schools need to ensure that the food consumed by children on school premises (at the cafeteria or in a school mess) follow stringent measures and guidelines to maintain hygiene. Food served at schools must undergo regular quality checks to ensure that the food is fit for consumption.

SAFETY & SECURITY ANCHOR

#10

Smartphone technology can be used to a school's advantage to maintain the safety and security of students. Check for the research adoption of using BLOCKCHAIN Technology to protect students within the campus. The use of AI and Augmented Reality is also on the cards. Technology adoption is hence a requisite for running a school peacefully.

SAFETY & SECURITY ANCHOR

#11

Install EFFECTIVE CCTV Cameras in all Nooks and Corners of the School Premises, including the entry of the WASHROOMS and entry/ exit points of the

school. **It is suggested to be installed in** *every classroom, and the parents should be given access to the feed through a mobile phone app.*

SAFETY & SECURITY ANCHOR

#12

The School Compound Should Be Fenced and Gated. Guards should be on ROUND duty with proper LATHIS and TORCH with a whistle. The respective locations of these guards should be monitored using the GPRS tracking system.

SAFETY & SECURITY ANCHOR

#13

There Should Be Security Personal Stationed at the School Gate and must MONITOR the CCTV Camera on the round. The Entry/ Exit REGISTER should be marked and duly signed regularly for ENTRY and EXIT.

SAFETY & SECURITY ANCHOR

#14

Clearance Should Be Given to Any Visitor before Entering the School Premises by the person responsible for the MEETING. *Teachers must stand guard in front of classroom doors, regularly watching for misconduct during the Parent/ Teacher Meetings.*

SAFETY & SECURITY ANCHOR

#15

Students and Workers Should Always Be In Possession of their ID cards and valid security IDs. *Police officers need to be given the authority to conduct random pre-emptive searches of students' lockers and personal property. A check on driving licenses and vehicles need to be monitored as well.*

SAFETY & SECURITY ANCHOR

#16

Proper Security Check Must Be Conducted Before Employing Teachers and Other Employees. Schools must conduct periodic criminal history checks of school employees during their employment. In addition, the school must establish policies requiring school employees to report any arrests for crimes to their school employees within 24 hours of such arrests.

SAFETY *&* SECURITY ANCHOR

#17

Students Should Be Trained On Security Related Subjects/ incidences/ scenario. The school must be a place in practice where students develop both socially and emotionally. Staff members and the students should know WHAT TO DO IN A CRISIS? There has to be a collaboration with the POLICE.

SAFETY *&* SECURITY ANCHOR

#18

A Leadership Team and a Security Club Should Be Formed in the School with REGULAR safety and security guidelines. The team should include all types of individuals from the school, community and others. These individuals should develop school-wide prevention plans, analyse the needs assessment, and formulate short and long term goals.

SAFETY & SECURITY ANCHOR

#19

Only the Parents of Students or Someone Duly Assigned Should Be Allowed to Pickup Students from the School. Staff must be trained to recognise the parents, and their training ensures understanding, support and use of a school-wide violence prevention plan. The constant movement makes the students and the faculty comfortable with the crisis plan.

SAFETY & SECURITY ANCHOR

#20

Central Security Alarm Should Be Installed in the School Premises. A mock drill for the same must be carried out from time to time. There have to be a complete 360 degree of integrated security solution from intrusion detection security systems, video surveillance and fire alarm test and inspections to mass notification, emergency communication, an indication of any Terrorist Attack and everything in between.

SAFETY & SECURITY ANCHOR

#21

Students' Bags Should Be Searched from Time to Time to Prevent Them from Bringing Dangerous Weapons into the School. These random searches must be based on unique, school-wide needs to ensure school safety and should be truly random. A random search can not be done to target any individual child in the school.

SAFETY *&* SECURITY ANCHOR

#22

Students' Activities should be strictly monitored to prevent them from Joining Secret Cults. Individual traits of the children need to be monitored, and constant positive reinforcement and motivation need to be given. This is possible only if the child feels connected to the Teacher. Monitoring activates the possibility for classroom development.

SAFETY *&* SECURITY ANCHOR

#23

Students Should Be Encouraged To Report any Suspicious Moves or Persons within the School Premises to the School Management. Teachers should connect with other teachers who interact with the child in the next grade and help work on the child's developmental process. We must provide various reporting options like anonymous reporting strategies through websites, text, phones and designated teachers, counsellors and peers on priority.

SAFETY & SECURITY ANCHOR

#24

Students Should Only Be Allowed To Leave the School Premises Only When They Have a Pass from the Security Post. No child should be allowed to walk home without prior consent from a parent or guardian. Parents must understand that it is their responsibility of, theirs' and not the school, once their children have left the school premises.

SAFETY *&* SECURITY ANCHOR

#25

People Should Be Discouraged from Loitering or Parking Their Cars outside the School fence. The schools should encourage parents to adopt the carpool system to drop and pick up their children. This may reduce traffic chaos outside schools and ease the flow of vehicles. The priority is to gel with the society/ public/ neighbourhood injunction for ease of business and transit within the framework of security.

SAFETY *&* SECURITY ANCHOR

#26

The use of mobile phones in school settings or environments is a topic of debate. Students Should Not Be Allowed to Make Use of Mobile Phones within the School Premises. There should not be any BLANKET Ban on phones, but when in emergencies, the children should be allowed to use. They should only have access to a mobile phone where there is a need to contact parents/ guardians in an emergency.

SAFETY *&* SECURITY ANCHOR

#27

Students and PARENTS Should Be Issued Access Cards with BIO-METRIC system and recognition. This system can be used for the purchase of food and drink in the dining hall and for the use in the library to manage the loan of books and submission of books issued earlier using the recognition.

SAFETY & SECURITY ANCHOR

#28

Kids Should Be Taught Not to Talk to Strangers within or even outside the school campus. The unfortunate incidents about abductions and molestations in and outside the schools with our students makes it more important to educate our kids about Mr. Danger Stranger and how and why they should continue to be vigilant all their life.

SAFETY & SECURITY ANCHOR

#29

Teach teachers To Be Vigilant on issues related to CYBER Bullying, CHILD Abuse and Racism. Child Abuse Identification and Reporting workshop is essential. The Child Abuse Identification & Reporting Workshop must be a priority for both the PARENTS and the Faculty. Care should be taken in asking, and deciphering kids' reactions to, inquiries regarding signs of misuse. Similar contemplations apply when a youngster makes a charge of misuse, or volunteers data which adds up to that. In certain conditions,

conversing with the kid will rapidly explain beginning worries into a doubt that misuse has happened, and highlight the requirement for a quick reference. Staff ought to know that the manner by which they converse with a kid can affect the proof which is put forward assuming there are resulting criminal procedures, and the degree of addressing ought to, in this manner, be kept to a base: As a priority, Online wellbeing implies acting and remaining safe while utilizing computerized innovations. It is more extensive than basically web innovation and incorporates electronic correspondence by means of text messages, social conditions and applications, and utilizing games consoles through any advanced gadget. In all cases, in schools and somewhere else, it is a foremost concern.

SAFETY & SECURITY ANCHOR

#30

Teach the school's emergency procedures via **YOUTUBE** *Videos/ Simulation Games/ Mock Drills as a part of* **ROUTINE** *exercise. Children should know how to respond to any* **EMERGENCY**. *Online drills sessions must be there on* **SUPW** *periods in common as an exercise in practice.*

SAFETY *&* SECURITY ANCHOR

#31

Teach the Travel Routes to and from the school for near by locations. POICE and relief/ help/ emergency numbers must be land marked and earmarked at every nook and corner of the school around the campus and children and staff should be pro-active for any assistance.

SAFETY *&* SECURITY ANCHOR

#32

All stakeholders need to be well versed about the school security and safety measures. A regular orientation towards any new building and exit and entry plans should be mentioned via exclusive videos and manuals to all the stake holders to face any emergency. Most importantly, Twenty-first Century life presents risks including savagery, prejudice, radicalisation and above all, the abuse. While youngsters and youngsters should be safeguarded from these risks, they likewise should be instructed about how to perceive and stay away from the dangers, in age suitable way. Understudies need to know how to adapt assuming that they go over improper material or circumstances on the web and ought to be urged to look for help and counsel when they need it unafraid of rebuke or criminalisation. It becomes so more so over, that the Schools likewise need to perform risk evaluations on the advances inside their school to guarantee that they are completely mindful of and can moderate the potential dangers implied with their utilization. The

ideas has to be explore the spectrum and manage the attentive and obvious concern of safety at large.

SAFETY & SECURITY ANCHOR

#33

Overall, it is the <u>environment</u> that is the biggest enabler of learning. It can be created by focussing on 3 major components- the teachers, the technologies and the curriculum. Teacher training is the <u>key component</u> of Finland Model along with the creative and customized curriculum. The "one size fits all" Indian system of education and rote memory based exam only produces parrots, not creative thinkers.

SAFETY & SECURITY ANCHOR

#34

Staff must be informed periodically on Student Safety and Behavioural Issues. The teachers should not limit their interaction with a class for a year but track the development of the children as they move on. the whole process of teaching and learning should be immersed *in a "facilitating" environment which is not very easy to create. Just look at the home environment. It is all about control and command. This is where our children get started. Hence home, school environment and social values have to be in sync to produce Finland system.*

SAFETY & SECURITY ANCHOR

#35

Any Loose Electrical Wires must be tended to immediately. The admin/ staff/ prefect/ member of the student council on floor duty must inform the concerned authority towards any short circuit or loose wiring in the campus of any kind.

SAFETY & SECURITY ANCHOR

#36

Regular structural audits must be conducted of the school building. There has to be a timely inspection of FIRE ALARMS/ FIRE FIGHTING EQUIPMENTS to be in place and in working order to handle any emergency. This must be tested via MOCK Drills on and off.

SAFETY & SECURITY ANCHOR

#37

*The Schools must assure the railings and pathways to be sturdy along the staircase and corridors. They must be well lit and guarded by an Adult during dispersal. Wherever practical, separate access points should be provided for people and vehicles to ensure the **safe** flow of both to and from the **school** boundary.*

Right from the the fencing around its perimeter to the main entrance gates, a visitor gets a clear impression of a schools' commitment to safety and security well before entering its grounds.

SAFETY & SECURITY ANCHOR

#38

***Toilets** at **school** ensure privacy and **safety**. Going to a **school** lacking proper basic facilities, like **toilets**, could be one of the most frustrating situations for many hence the entrance to the TOILETS need to be monitored. Every move of the student around the un-*

manned/ restricted places must be observed and checked using the CCTV Camera.

SAFETY & SECURITY ANCHOR

#39

School ID **cards** are intended to identify an elementary, high **school**, or college **student**, in order to prove their membership of the **school** or college.

Badges and name tags must be made mandatory for the TEACHING and NON-TEACHING STAFF. Assure meeting up of the SOCIAL and EMOTIONAL needs of the children through PEP talk and interactions and may include HOME VISITS by the teachers.

SAFETY & SECURITY ANCHOR

#40

Police Verification of the Teaching and Non-Teaching Staff should always be undertaken. This may include checking of the Cultural and Parental Background of the stake holders too as a documented information. Ensuring employment of support staff only from authorised agencies and maintenance of proper records, is another one of the guidelines.

SAFETY & SECURITY ANCHOR

#41

CBSE Quote

""Schools must get psychometric evaluation done for all the staff. Such verification and evaluation for non-teaching staff -such as bus drivers, conductors, peons and other support staff -may be done very carefully and in a detailed manner,"

Psychometric Evaluation of the Teaching and Non-Teaching Staff should always be undertaken.

SAFETY & SECURITY ANCHOR

#42

The playground should be aesthetically designed and maintained regularly with opportunities for multi courts and games with Physical Activities at all levels. Assure marking of every child's attendance to be marked thrice a day and messages sent to parents if their children are absent. Assure No child should be punished in such a way that could cause mental or physical trauma.

SAFETY & SECURITY ANCHOR

#43

The classrooms must be aesthetically designed with equipped ICT facilities and support mechanism. Regularly update licenses for the software in use with proper use of anti-virus and a check on CYBER bullying with FIRE WALLS installed in systems.

SAFETY & SECURITY ANCHOR

#44

A check on having enough TOILETS separately for girls and boys/ Male and Female Staff, safe drinking water, medical room and counselling room. Among the precautionary measures suggested for girls' safety are separate washrooms for boys and girls, at a suitable distance, and deployment of a female attendant in the girls' washroom.

SAFETY & SECURITY ANCHOR

\#45

All the students must be given Psychiatric Support and Counselling particularly on Cyber Bullying.

School counsellors should teach sex education classes, provide information to students about bullying and offer seminars on study skills.

They MUST work in collaboration with the teachers, parents and special educators to create a healthy learning environment that makes them feel comfortable.

SAFETY & SECURITY ANCHOR

#46

Busses should follow clear mandates different factor including the seat to student ratio, display of emergency numbers and tracking system. A female teacher or attendant should accompany a girl if she must leave the school for an exam or another event, and the school bus female attendant should not leave the bus unless the last girls are dropped to their destination.

SAFETY & SECURITY ANCHOR

#47

Aesthetically designed furniture should be in place, age appropriate wise in classrooms as per different levels. The school building should be designed for natural light and ventilation in flow.

SAFETY & SECURITY ANCHOR

#48

A school safety committee should be constituted to ensure and monitor safety practices within the school. Student Council should be directed to shoulder the additional responsibility towards safety and security of the students. The school must also have a vigilance committee comprising parents and the schools should follow it.

SAFETY & SECURITY ANCHOR

#49

Visit to the Police Station by the schools' kids to understand the role of police in our daily life and their contribution to the safety and security of the citizens of the country. Schools need to take cognisance of safety issues as per the guidelines set by the boards and the government.

SAFETY & SECURITY ANCHOR

#50

There has to be a regular METAL DETECTOR CHECK for Visitors. Assure school stakeholders are frequently trained to manage emergencies and disasters with adequate practice in conducting mock drills and evacuation drills.

SAFETY & SECURITY ANCHOR

#51

There has to be a documented Safety Norm for every LABORATORY in the school. Check for the availability of facilities supporting differently abled students. Students should never ever work in science lab in the absence of their teachers. Students must be made to wear safety goggles, lab coat, and shoes in the science laboratory. Loose clothes, sandals, and open hairs should be a strict NO in school science labs.

SAFETY & SECURITY ANCHOR

#52

Every student in the school and the teacher/ employee must know how to operate a fire fighting Equipment installed in the campus. Identify the TWO closest exits and all possible evacuation routes. Know locations of **fire** *alarms and how to use them. Teachers and Students must report vandalized* **fire equipment** *to campus security.*

SAFETY & SECURITY ANCHOR

#53

Regular Inspections of Fire Fighting Equipment must be on cards. Assure stringent provisions for emergency management are in place for all types of FIRE and alarm during emergency and call for nearest POLICE STATIONS and mention of important PHONE NUMBERS in place.

SAFETY & SECURITY ANCHOR

#54

The Annual Curriculum plan of the school should integrate academic, social, physical and emotional needs of the children. Identify what hazards are likely to affect the area in and around your school. Determine the severity of impact of each identified hazard. Students and staff must be trained how to use the plan and what their responsibilities will be in a given response.

SAFETY & SECURITY ANCHOR

#55

The infrastructure including Computer Labs, Science Labs, Math Labs must be appropriate and meet expected standards ALL THE TIME. Areas where students congregate while waiting for buses and associated pedestrian paths are adequate to avoid overcrowding. Access into each building is controllable through designated entry points. If possible, identify one entry point for visitors.

SAFETY & SECURITY ANCHOR

#56

The school has to have adequate medical facilities and should be equipped with a nurse/ doctor to handle medical and other emergencies. Create at least one Administrator Emergency Tool Kit for each school building. Develop and distribute emergency response guides for each classroom. Establish and document procedures for providing access to mental health services for students and staff.

SAFETY & SECURITY ANCHOR

#57

Rest rooms, toilets, laboratory, playground, classrooms must be CLEAN, AIRY and WELL maintained. Schools must also have ramps and need to admit students of disadvantaged groups and should also have SPECIAL Educators to assist the needy concerned. Send at least two girls/ boys to the washroom at a time, so that in case of an emergency, one of them can raise an alarm.

SAFETY & SECURITY ANCHOR

#58

There should be separate TOILETS for Female and Male Staff. The school must also assure having adequate medical facilities and should be equipped to handle medical and other emergencies. Without proper cleaning, washrooms can become breeding grounds for germs that can spread disease throughout the school population.

SAFETY & SECURITY ANCHOR

#59

The Library should be airy and be equipped with EMERGENCY Alarm System and Fire Fighting Equipment. Use posters and bulleting boards to emphasize potential dangers and safety procedures. Post legible, accurate emergency numbers and procedures.

SAFETY & SECURITY ANCHOR

#60

The school must take initiative to Conservation of Environment and should also take MAJOR initiatives on IMPLEMENTING Waste Management Practices. Use organic waste for composting and teach students about how it works. Schools can use the compost on the school gardens, saving on the cost of fertiliser and other chemicals. Schools could set up worm farms, which can be used to teach parts of the curriculum.

SAFETY *&* SECURITY ANCHOR

#61

*The school should have a provision for DIFFERENTLY ABLED INDIVIDUALS and should provide conducive working environment with growth opportunities. Students in **wheelchairs** attend public **schools** more and more regularly. Schools must adhere to the norms for provision of assistance to these children.*

SAFETY & SECURITY ANCHOR

#62

There has to be sense of SAFETY and SECURITY in the School with regular evacuation drills being carried out from time to time.

Ref: Quote: Example

Fire Drill PM, #5 of 5, School Year 2016-2017 3.21.17 @ 1:40 PM Evacuation/Shelter Time: 1min, 00sec Participants: 45 total participants Drill Conducted by: Loretta Tobolske-Horn, Greenfield Principal Acknowledgement of Completed Drill: On File at HCISD Office, 310 W. Bacon Street, Hillsdale

SAFETY & SECURITY ANCHOR

#63

Schools Need an eye beyond CCTV Cameras. A must checks by teachers and knowing each child by first name is very important. In addition, there has to be a HEALTH CARD for every child with all MEDICAL records in count.

SAFETY & SECURITY ANCHOR

#64

Schools must ensure all records in the school diary should be updated and recorded for easy reference. Parents must be communicated about their child's health issues, what so ever on PRIORITY.

"Nevertheless, no school can work well for children if parents and teachers do not act in partnership on behalf of the children's best interests. Parents have every right to understand what is happening to their children at school, and teachers have the responsibility to share that......" : - Dorothy Cohen

SAFETY & SECURITY ANCHOR

#65

The schools should advocate, model and teach safe, legal, and ethical use of digital information and technology; promote and model responsible social interaction related to the use of technology and information; celebrate Cyber Security Week and conduct activities to create awareness through cyber clubs.

SAFETY & SECURITY ANCHOR

#66

Check the Cyber Bulling If any through ONE on ONE interactions and observatory efforts. Frequent CYBER ethics sessions need to be observed and organised for the students, parents and other stake holders. There has to be a digital technology program in place like ERP which should serve as an interactive medium 'between the educators and the guardians"

SAFETY & SECURITY ANCHOR

#67

Check on CHILD ABUSE in practice using friendly options with the students by asking them to share the uncomfortable moments they feel being around in the school. **It is up to all of us to ensure our children grow up in the environments that build confidence, friendship, security and happiness, irrespective their family circumstances or backgrounds. Keeping children safe from harm requires a vigilant and informed community.**

SAFETY & SECURITY ANCHOR

#68

Check on SECURITY agency people with their I-Cards, Lathis, Umbrella, Torch and Safety Belts in place. There has to be a fitness MEDICAL certificate available for all guards on duty.

SAFETY *&* SECURITY ANCHOR

#69

Any water logging in the wash room or around the wash room/ corridors. A check required on priority. Well-designed **school restrooms** can enhance student health, deter misbehavior, and conserve resources. The initiative should be that the children will than bring these behaviours home with them, thereby acting as agents of change in their communities.

SAFETY *&* SECURITY ANCHOR

#70

Floors surfaces chipped or carpets in Music Rooms worn out with spots or holes may lead sudden slipping of the children and dis balancing. **Safety precautions** peculiar to any new lesson should be emphasised at the start of the lesson.

SAFETY *&* SECURITY ANCHOR

#71

Observe if the Aisles are free of boxes, waste baskets, chairs and other obstacles that may impede traffic within the campus. Check on the internal flooring of the classroom, lighting in the classroom and the children are aware of the evacuation drill and the classroom is naturally ventilated. The classrooms must and ideally should have rules towards letting the students set their own climate of respect and responsibility.

SAFETY & SECURITY ANCHOR

#72

Check on whether the doors have stoppers in classrooms. Students must check on their behaviours and Teachers must help students correct their behaviors, help them understand violating the rules results in consequences. They should be told to respect ground rules and the kids should feel free to discuss issues without fear.

SAFETY & SECURITY ANCHOR

#73

Check on POWER sockets in classrooms, if any, must be out of the reach of the children. Assure proper Earth wire towards protection against electric shock. The children should be told to stand clear of any fallen power lines. Remove unused wall outlets and apply tape over unused plug holes or cord holders. Also ensure they get dry when the come out of the swimming pools in the classrooms to operate computers or any electrical device in particular.

SAFETY & SECURITY ANCHOR

#74

*Five S in action with special marking for FAN (F), TUBE (T) as special mentions on switch boards within classrooms. A check update required. 5S is a workplace organization method that uses a list of **five** Japanese words: seiri, seiton, seiso, seiketsu, and shitsuke. These have been translated as "Sort", "Set In Order", "Shine", "Standardize" and "Sustain"*

SAFETY & SECURITY ANCHOR

#75

Evaluate the MEDICAL history of the students' time to time and teachers must study the child's health record as a part of the routine. He or she must have a record of the food allergy, physical disability or if there is a cause or a case of bullying, with a keep of the information conveyed to the Head of the school and the Principal in the loop.

SAFETY & SECURITY ANCHOR

#76

Are Staircases well lit?

"You can't study or learn if you don't feel safe at school."

—Bill Jelkin, director of Student Services, Millard Public Schools (Omaha, Neb.)

The school MUST have an EMERGENCY plan A and B and MUST not be making decisions under DURESS that they have not practiced.

"Students not only understand 'see something, say something,' but they also know who to tell and feel comfortable approaching them."

—Rex Barrett, acting director of security services, Prince George's County (Md.) Public Schools

SAFETY & SECURITY ANCHOR

#77

Are Staircases free from litter, spills or clutter? Assure children travel on the right side of staircases and hallways. Appealing staircases will encourage use. The teachers and the incharges must monitor slops and falls, sharp edges and the assurance of up to date maintenance.

SAFETY & SECURITY ANCHOR

#78

Do Teachers or Students stand on some stand or ladders in any case for teaching/ demonstrating which needs supervision and support. If need be, the assistance from students can be a support but under supervision. This is practical real life learning and experience to them.

SAFETY & SECURITY ANCHOR

#79

Do Students/ Teachers RUN in the area after assembly or during the getting over of the school? A must check and solution drawn for an easy and an organised exit and entry to the assembly ground. The students should be guided during the dispersal. There has to be a public-address system to ensure timely and safe evacuation during an emergency.

SAFETY & SECURITY ANCHOR

#80

Children should be briefed about safe touch and unsafe touch, about avoiding interaction with strangers and reporting any and every concern, however irrelevant it may seem. Also any change in behaviour has to be communicated to the parents. There has to be an open channels of communication with the students and they should be give a patient hearing for even smallest of matters.

SAFETY & SECURITY ANCHOR

#81

The buses and other school transport should be IDENTITY marked with help line phone numbers and students should be issued a Bus Badge with Bus Route Number. They should use only the allotted bus and bus stop. Boarding and alighting from bus should be done in silence and in an orderly manner.

SAFETY & SECURITY ANCHOR

#82

Computers and SERVERS need supervision in LABS/ deserted rooms. Passwords and WIFI should be protected and activated timely for execution. Original Software should be preferred to assure attack of Malware or Virus in particular. Students should not be allowed to use external drives.

SAFETY & SECURITY ANCHOR

#83

No Strangers should be allowed to Meet Children. No stranger, driver or a family friend should be allowed to pick the children up. The Principals' helpline should be used to inform any irregularity. Students should not be allowed to drive motorized vehicles such as cars, scooters and motorcycles within or outside the school.

SAFETY & SECURITY ANCHOR

#84

Do all employees know the exit locations and directions when in EMERGENCY? EAP or Emergency Assembly Points should be located away from the building. Fire Exit Symbols should be in place for immediately evacuation using the nearest escape route. The schools must ENSURE School Building Level Emergency Preparedness and Response Plan.

SAFETY & SECURITY ANCHOR

#85

Are fire drills conducted regularly? Check on Training of Task Forces, Demonstration, Mock Drills, develop emergency resource contact inventory for human resource, transport and tools required dealing with emergency response, Hazard Hunt Programmes, Training for First Aid Search and Rescue in addition to building evacuation drills on a regular basis. It is recommended to prepare a floor wise detailed evacuation plan and conduct mock drill for earthquake or a fire to test emergency plans and update the findings.

SAFETY & SECURITY ANCHOR

#86

Assure a QUICK background check of visitors in the schools and information explored via IDs'. Involve PARENTS as partners to Safety and Security Mechanism in action. Assure Disaster Management in Education and formal training/ workshop for all the stakeholders to mainstream the discipline of disaster risk management.

SAFETY & SECURITY ANCHOR

#87

Are all incidents/ accidents properly reported, investigated and documented? Check on provision to parents the information on school's emergency policies and procedures to further update on Emergency Notification Cards in the almanacs. The plans must execute as an EMERGENCY plan and keeping the students safe when crisis strikes.

SAFETY & SECURITY ANCHOR

#88

Is medical help readily available? Assure procedure to evacuate the building, evacuate the premises, shift to temporary shelter, safeguard students and staff, notify parents, notify media, provide transportation and debrief procedures timely and appropriately. Make available the important PHONE numbers in case of emergency to be painted on display around the campus.

SAFETY & SECURITY ANCHOR

#89

Enhancements. All in the name of safety with employees need to be empowered to check and identify any uncommon person. School must appoint a PRO or a public information officer to provide information and the current status of the situation to the parents and other inquiring parties in case of an emergency.

SAFETY & SECURITY ANCHOR

#90

VISIOTORS Batch to be given to all who wish to come to the school during office hours. Also assure the emergency plans need to be reviewed and revised regularly. Make it a living document with modifications as a requisite timely. The document should address prevention/ mitigation, preparedness, response and recovery aspects in particular.

SAFETY & SECURITY ANCHOR

#91

Assure conducting a preliminary assessment of preparedness measures of each school building. There has to be a review of the building layout and the surrounding areas for safe evacuation of the students. Also inspect equipment to ensure it operates during crisis situations. Develop a command structure for responding to an emergency.

SAFETY & SECURITY ANCHOR

#92

Assure children walk on the side off the corridors to assure everyone to get to classes safely. Make sure the good plans are never finished. They need to be always updated based on the experience and changing vulnerabilities and assessment of current capabilities. One must carry out shelter assessment needs for various situational responses. An emergency supply inventory should be checked and updated as per the expiry.

SAFETY & SECURITY ANCHOR

#93

Assure children and any adult, RESPECT, if some one has an injury, excuse not to get in their way of walking. One must be aware and prepared, not SCARED should be the priority. Every room in the school should have a map posted identifying two ways out. The exit paths should be obvious and kept free of obstruction.

SAFETY & SECURITY ANCHOR

#94

Follow rules to go up and down the stairs. During an emergency, once every one has safely exited the building, they should remain outside at a predetermined location until the 'all clear' green signal has been given to enter the building again.

SAFETY & SECURITY ANCHOR

#95

Include TERRORISM THREAT in School Syllabi as a priority. All schools up to the secondary level should include this as a very critical issue in their syllabi. It should be as compulsory for students as the military service, which is mandatory for the youths in Israel. This is a security step towards safety and security scenario within schools.

SAFETY & SECURITY ANCHOR

#96

Assure and Make Sure there is a SILENCE ZONE in the school to monitor and assure discipline. Let the staff and students follow the same religiously. Quiet Zones in schools and classrooms are an easy way to help meet a need that all students have at one time or another. The need to be able to take a break from the noise and pressure of social interaction and recharge.

SAFETY & SECURITY ANCHOR

#97

Let the children play SMART and follow the elementary playground safely. Let the children follow for their turns in line. Assure attention by the teachers on swings, slides and other equipment. They must actively supervise students on play grounds. Assure age appropriate play ground equipment. The children should only be allowed in proper attire and choose playground with shock absorbing surfaces.

SAFETY & SECURITY ANCHOR

#98

Do you have a designated drop off and pick up area at your school? A defined pick up and drop points for walkers, bus takers and Parents' fetch & drop. The guided line wise provision has to be a routine for normal dispersal on all days and special provisions for the raining/ emergency days accordingly. Specified Drop-offs spots are locations in the proximity of primary schools where parents can drop off or pick up their child.

SAFETY & SECURITY ANCHOR

#99

Are safety rules clearly displayed and visible?

Check the updates on Step up for Students' Health, promoting a healthy school ecosystem. The schools need to provide a monthly calendar for educating each child on topics such as hygiene, nutrition, stress and vision through educational videos and hands on activities integrated via guest lectures and workshops.

SAFETY & SECURITY ANCHOR

#100

It is so very important of the fact that the schools can't cover each situation and that guardians have to ultimately have the essential obligation regarding the security and shielding of their kids. It is suggested that schools, such a long ways as is sensibly conceivable, draw in with guardians to share data, counsel and direction on the suitable and safe utilization of advanced innovation. This goes a long way in managing the schools effectively and winning the heards of the Heads of Schools in particular.

II

Safeguarding the kids in Schools

Everyone in education keeps children and young people safe from harm and abuse. All staff in a school, both teaching and non-teaching, have a responsibility to ensure the protection and welfare of children is paramount. This also extends to any volunteers accepted to work in the school during school hours when pupils are on the premises. As a best practice, in the children's best interests, and as a support for the Designated Teachers, the school should establish a Safeguarding Team. A youngster needing security is a kid in danger of or prone to experience critical hurt, which can be ascribed to an individual or people or association, either by a demonstration of commission or exclusion, or a youngster who has endured or is experiencing critical hurt. 'Hurt' signifies abuse or the disability of wellbeing or advancement, and the question of whether the damage is not entirely settled as per different approaches by the public authority. Teachers will have access to a range of age-appropriate

and evaluated resources to support the teaching of sensitive subjects.

Schools are expected to do whatever is reasonable, in all the circumstances of the case, to safeguard and promote their pupils' safety and wellbeing. Every school should work to create and maintain an ethos that contributes to the care, safety and wellbeing of children or young people and must maintain a child protection policy that reflects both its legal duties and its safeguarding and child protection responsibilities.

Public consciousness of issues connecting with defending and kid assurance proceeds to develop, as the entire setting quickly extends because of changes in the public eye and, especially, innovation. Late shielding and youngster insurance cases have featured the need for everybody to take more time for safeguarding kids and the need for those in critical situations to have a reasonable comprehension of their job in sticking to approaches and methodology. In particular, a school's child protection policy must be a 'living document' providing a secure framework within which all staff can work. It reflects the values to which the school community is committed and how the school is fulfilling its statutory responsibilities in safeguarding children.

Shielding is more than youngster security. Defending starts with safeguard schooling and exercises that empower kids and youngsters to grow up securely, safely in conditions where their turn of events and prosperity is advanced. It incorporates backing to families and early mediation to address the issues of youngsters and go on through to kid assurance, which alludes explicitly to the action that is attempted to safeguard individual youngsters or youngsters who are enduring, or liable to stay hurt.

The accompanying standards ought to support all methodologies, approaches, methodology, practices; furthermore, administrations connect with protecting youngsters and youngsters. The youngster or youngster's government assistance is foremost - The government assistance of the kid is the central thought for the courts and in childcare practice. A suitable equilibrium ought to be struck between the youngster's privileges and parents'.

All endeavours ought to be made to work co-operatively with guardians, except if
doing so is conflicting with guaranteeing the youngster's wellbeing. In addition to it, the voice of the kid or youngster ought to be heard. Children and youngsters reserve a privilege to be heard, paid attention to, and taken indeed, assessing their age and understanding. They ought to be counselled and engaged with all matters and choices that might influence their lives and be furnished with practical help to do so where that is required. Where possible and fitting, movement ought to be embraced with the permission of the kid or youngster and, where conceivable, to accomplish their favoured result.

The observations reveal that the Parents are upheld to practice parental obligation and families assisted with remaining together - Parents have liability regarding their youngsters rather than freedoms over them. In certain conditions, guardians will share parental responsibility with others like other carers or legal specialists.

Activities taken by associations ought to, where it is to the most significant advantage of the youngster, offer proper help to assist families with remaining together. This is regularly the most effective way to develop the existence chances of kids and youngsters and give them the best results for their future.

Safeguarding is a joint obligation, and the best approach to guaranteeing that a youngster's necessities are met is working in the organisation. Quality direction relies upon the most conceivable comprehension of the kid or youngster's conditions and requirements. This includes successful data sharing, solid authoritative administration and initiative, cooperation and understanding between families, organisations, people and experts.

The significance of forestalling issues happening or deteriorating through the presentation of ideal solid measures by the schools in particular. Children ought to be secure in general, and in conditions where a parent or carer isn't addressing their necessities, they ought to be safeguarded by the State. It is always preferable to prevent abuse or for intervention to take place at the earliest possible stage. Through their day-to-day contact with individual children, school staff, especially teachers, and non-teaching staff, including lunch-time supervisors and ancillary or auxiliary staff, are particularly well placed to observe outward symptoms, change in appearance, behaviour, learning pattern or development.

Evidence-based and informed navigation - Decisions and activities should be thought of very much educated and in light of results required to assess the youngster's particular conditions, dangers to which they are uncovered, and their surveyed needs. The essential obligation regarding defending and insurance of youngsters rests with guardians who ought to have reasonable expectations about raising any worries they have corresponding to their kid. As a feature of the continuous work of cultivating trust and significant associations with guardians/carers, the school ought to help guardians/carers to comprehend its liability regarding the government assistance of the multitude of kids and youngsters in its charge.

All approaches, including youngster assurance, peaceful consideration against tormenting, positive way of behaving, online security, and objections, should be given to guardians/carers at intake. The kid security strategy ought to be audited and yet again given, at the very least, every two years as a periodic safety and security action plan within schools.

A priority on types of abuses and the concern!

To the surprise of many, Neglect, which is the inability to accommodate a youngster's necessities, whether it be adequate food, clothing, cleanliness, oversight or a safe house, is probably going to result in the genuine disability of a kid's wellbeing or advancement. Kids frequently disregarded also experience the ill effects of different sorts of misuse.

Next comes Physical Abuse is purposely genuinely harming a kid. It could take a wide range of structures, including hitting, gnawing, squeezing, shaking, tossing, hurting, consuming or singing, suffocating or choking out a kid.

The other one is Sexual Abuse which happens when others use and take advantage of kids physically for their delight or gain or the satisfaction of others. Sexual maltreatment may include actual contact, including an attack by infiltration (for instance, assault, or on the other hand, oral sex) or non-penetrative demonstrations like masturbation, kissing, scouring and contacting outside attire. It might incorporate non-contact exercises, for example, including youngsters in creating sexual pictures, constraining kids to take a gander at sexual images or watch sexual practices, empowering youngsters to act in physically wrong ways or prepping a kid in anticipation of misuse (counting through e-innovation). Grown-up guys don't exclusively execute sexual maltreatment. Ladies can submit demonstrations of sexual abuse, as can different youngsters.

Next comes Emotional Abuse is the constant passionate abuse of a youngster. Moreover, it is called mental maltreatment, and it can have severe and determined unfavourable impacts on a kid's emotional turn of events. In addition, there is the prime importance of:

a. Guidance on Internet Use.

b. Advice on the safe use of the Internet and Digital Technologies.

c. Guidance on e-Safety Policy and Acceptable Use of the policy.

d. Dealing with Children with Increased Vulnerabilities

, e. The apparent need for the personal development curriculum requires schools to give specific attention to pupils' emotional wellbeing, health and safety, relationships, and the development of a moral thinking and value system as a priority.

III

The Post Pandemic Preparedness

As we know, learning online has become a more significant challenge for our kids in reality. The experts predict that the results will affect the learning outcome in years to come. We, as educators, are making a lot of effort in making learning visible, but we need a new model implementation. The interest to learn and teach post pandemics has prompted beneficial connections in people, advancements, societies, and enterprises. At the centre of instructing and teaching necessities lies a requirement for curiosity and interest in improvement.

Teaching is no such a place where there is no change at all. The whole teaching and learning platform have changed. The lethal pandemic has constrained humankind to advance and foster better approaches for bestowing instruction to understudies of all ages. Nobody will go to school except for everybody who is learning. Advancement has significantly changed how understudies are learning and educators are instructing. The development has overhauled everybody's perspectives about the world out there.

Available at AMAZON!

In the current period, the web is viewed as significantly heavenly. In contrast to a pen or furrow, it doesn't have a place with, nor is it solely utilised by its proprietor. The worldwide scenario uses it, and educators have acquired a more extensive effort with its assistance. During the startling disturbance of Covid-19, when individuals were shaken out of safe places, confusing things occurred in the advanced world. The change was taken well and adopted to the mechanism at pace. The closure of schools has made learning not at all speed but with the optional attribute in reality. It is now with the comfort of the home, the personal interest and the engagement, which vary from student to student.

Notwithstanding the lockdown requirements, educators have become more firmly associated worldwide and locally - on account of the magic of computerised innovations. More individuals can learn more subjects of their decision on the web, without hardly lifting a finger and opportunity, than previously. Educators from one side of the planet to the other have never been as interconnected, reliant, and intelligent as they are currently. Notwithstanding the recognisable domain of actual communications, computerised advances have talented instructors.

Another space of virtual exercise conveyance stretched to the vast majority. Online teaching and learning have created a lot of challenges. Managing the education for kids is a task to be evaluated now. Web-based showing presence hasn't been full-fledged and is going through progress. Robert Moore composes suitably, "In all types of distance educating, the capacity to adapt the relationship with far off students is significant." Following are a few things that educators can improve on the online stage as a part of the new age of learning and delivering teaching. These reflect the learning preface and allocate education as a priority in particular.

Gathering criticism and recovering from the same:

Educators should gather online education as a priority and, at the same time, look for its' criticism to distinguish what is and isn't working. The assessment of online teaching trends matters and ought to be offered influence to work on web-based learning.

This will persuade the online teaching by emphasising that the educator is intrigued and puts resources into every understudy. Students shouldn't feel that they are drawing with a Personal Computer. That may usually be an inclination of disconnectedness in web-based learning. They ought to be pulling in with one another, the educator, and the substance.

Show matters for the Students and Parents are of prime importance as well.

As likely interruptions encircle the home climate, keeping understudies connected with and propelled in their exercises is probably the most outstanding test instructors face while educating on the web. The show is vital to cause the understudies to feel about the newness of the climate. Instructors should be pleasantly spruced up alongside clean areas to have more coordinated conversations. On the off chance that understudies can see your face, it will be more spurring for them if you look drawn in and take interest with virtuous tolerance. Enlightening slide shows and recordings ought to have a decent picture quality.

The Instructors who educate in a similar tone can frequently make understudies feel exhausted and detached. Changing the manner of speaking to present new exercises or stirring up the rhythm can have constructive outcomes. Educators can work on narrating abilities and applause for all to hear. A solid web association with the coordinated substance before each class is likewise essential to working on the interest of understudies. The cloud connect is hence the responsibility of all the educators on priority. The concept of ORM- Online Reputation Management is *hence a requisite.*

Utilising innovation as a Priority

How should I teach? How to connect well with the students? All matters in the online spectrum and also in the actual classrooms. A broad scope of online devices, for example, whiteboards, printers, virtual games, content managers, drawing devices, record editors, breakout rooms, or screen sharing devices, can likewise cause understudies to remain alert. Examinations and allures can again have extraordinary positive outcomes. Turning up music or simply playing with various apparatuses can keep understudies quiet.

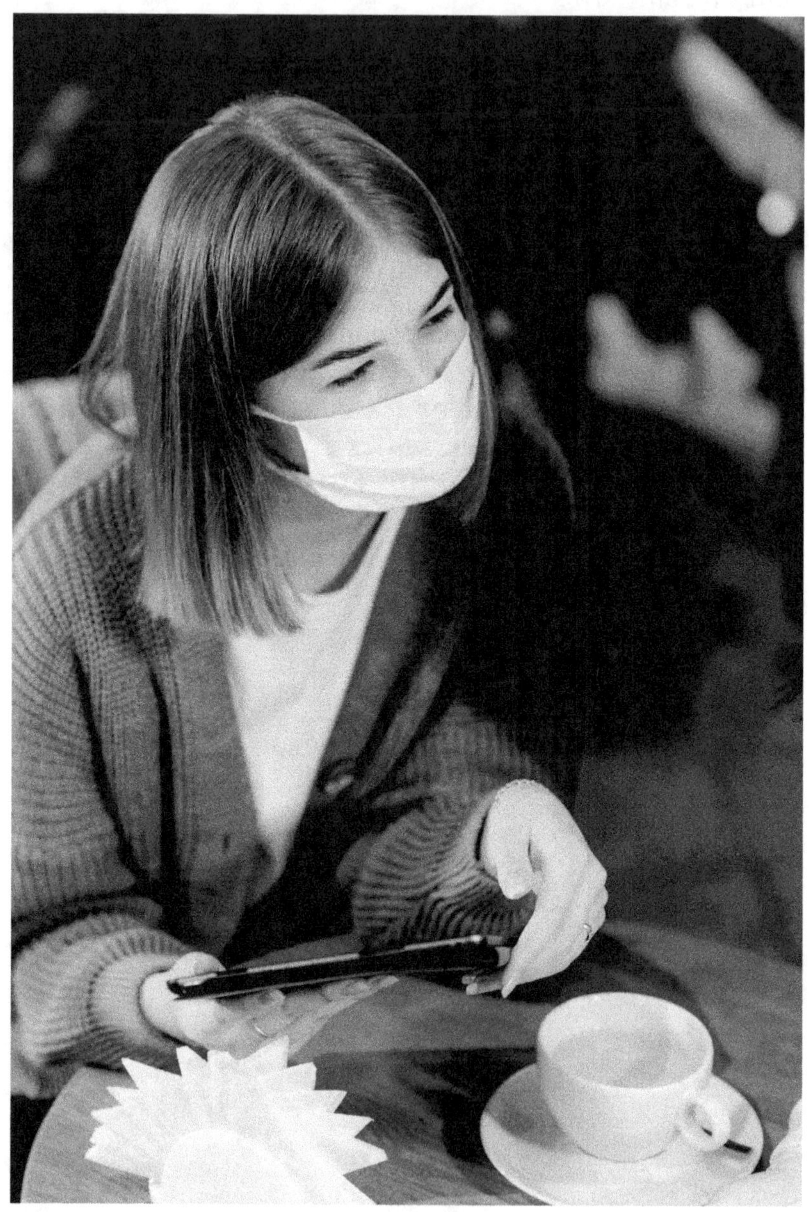

Defining objectives for a better learning outcome

The objectives as a takeaway, the objective as delivery and the learning outcome by the children all reflect an identity to explore learning in particular. Another approach to help the teaching methodology remains focused on their online examinations or assessment and is also required to cater to the defined objectives. Such a mechanism aids in helping them to remember their advancement. One straightforward approach to bringing transient dreams into the online study hall is to ensure every exercise has a straightforward layout that an instructor imparts to her understudies. Hence, they know where they are in the learning cycle and the setting for any movement they are doing. This will help the students to self-assess their advancement. Going excessively far into the future won't be decisive regarding long-haul objectives. Yet, instructors should have a go at setting aside time once in a while to check in with the understudies and put forward dreams together for the following month. As educators, we have to follow the spectrum with the new angle of teaching and learning. Here engaging the kids works wonders. It has to be part and parcel of every online classroom on priority.

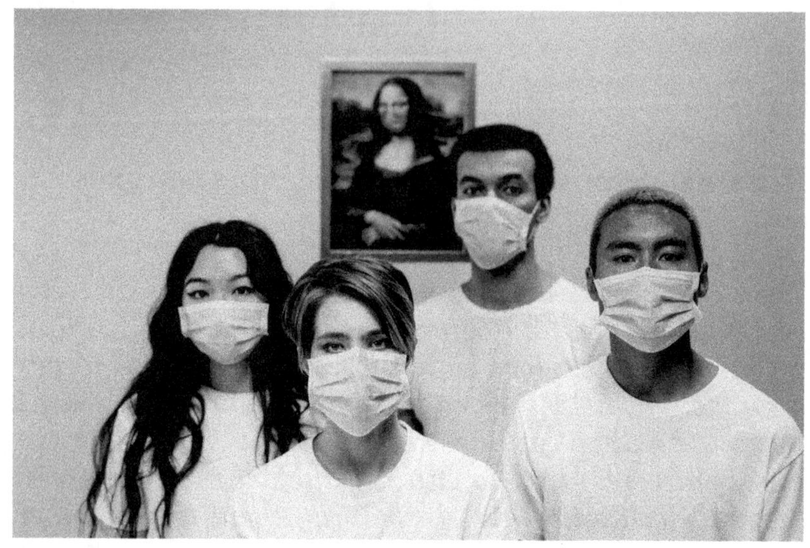

Keeping a connection with the environment

The educator's identity has changed with the march of the CORONA, and now it is like learning to learn as a new preface. We as educators need to explore the identity of more than just being the teacher but a learner. In a vis-à-vis class, it's run of the mill to give understudies some quiet reflection time to work alone or read content as extensive exercises don't interpret well in online homerooms. Long, thick messages are trying to peruse on a screen or available mobile tablets. Thus, quietness doesn't solve that well in virtual homerooms as it gives the ideal pardon to an understudy's regard for float somewhere else.

Hence, arranging exercises that keep understudies effectively clicking, composing, or talking through the training is the best approach for educators. Instructors can do this by posing heaps of inquiries, including games, and ensuring students need to do things like using attracting apparatuses or typing the discourse boxes.

From monitoring to giving instructions, assuring assignments all reflect at ease for the needful. We very well know that the pandemic has modelled the classroom learning to a new phase; a life without education for all the girls and boys is a life without any rights. While school closures are an effective precautionary measure to contain the spread of COVID-19, evidence from previous emergencies suggests that the longer children are unable to attend learning facilities, the more likely they will never return to school. This is a grave concern for all we, the educators today!

છ

IV

Learning In the VUCA World

Out of nowhere, I went over this word VUCA, Volatile, Uncertain, Complex, and Ambiguous, distinguishing the new world request of range with no decision except for an approach to confronting the difficulties changing over them into favourable circumstances.

Without a doubt, the world is confronting a difficult time today. Nobody was at any point arranged for this and will at any moment be. The need we the people must have a deduction today towards having a bunch of essential abilities, information and demeunour, and business purchases these at a cost.

Understanding the VUCA World, the better! The abbreviation VUCA - Volatile, Uncertain, Complex, and Ambiguous - was authored during the 1990s. It depicts numerous individuals' experiences of their work environment incredibly well.

In this sort of climate, it tends to be challenging to feel like you are adapting - not to mention flourishing. The abbreviation VUCA - Volatile, Uncertain, Complex, and Ambiguous - was instituted during the 1990s. It depicts numerous individuals' experiences of their work environment amazingly well. In the learning environment, the learners, particularly the students, need to come back to a supportive, friendly atmosphere, where their learning loss and socio-emotional needs are recognised, dwelled, and curated as per the new world order and acknowledged by the educators at large. These notions and craftings are required to help them get back on track. Let us revisit the fact that one of the key lessons learnt throughout the crisis is the importance of engaging parents and communities in pupils' learning process. And this must continue!

In this sort of climate, it may be not easy to feel like you are adapting - not to mention flourishing. Driving in a VUCA World - Leadership in the hours of Crisis is the new world order. We truly are seeing a remarkable change on the planet, and no part of our life is

immaculate by this change.

From the unexpected change in our way of life to the tremendous shift in mentality, the present circumstance has constrained us all to think fast, think extraordinary, and raise versatility. Professional life is the same. In the genuine sense, the world right currently exemplifies the VUCA reasoning; Volatile, Uncertain, Complex, and Ambiguous. We were not ready for this unexpected development, and many are confused about how to adapt to this and push forward. Convenient solutions will presently don't work; this change is somewhat perpetual.

It implies that we should rethink and re-adjust every technique for activity, thinking, acting, and being. Going ahead, mental and enthusiastic well-being balance has gotten basic on an ongoing premise. The capacity to re-adjust ranges of abilities, practices, and activities according to the progressions on the planet is a consuming worry for us all.

We are affected by this in some structure or the other. What is required is Mental Health, Resilience, Self consideration and inclusivity. On the off chance that organisations are unequipped for sympathy, we can venture up and connect with companions and family members in trouble. The Covid times require that extra portion of local area administration and social awareness for sure companions. We can start little—every single one of us. Keeping yourself propelled in any event, during the current situation where there is torment ..enduring ..passing .. lockdown.. dejection.. the world has halted. Inspiration comes from the inside.. equilibrium of the brain-body soul. In this infuriating situation, keep a quiet, adjusted, formed outlook .. keeping yourself propelled, self-inspired, and forcing others as the new practice.

"Keeping yourself roused in any event, during the current situation". Much as we like to consider these as reasonable and impartial and fearlessly take cutbacks in our step, the playing. At the point when an acquiring part loses his employment, the family's funds are seriously affected.

This is undoubtedly Sad and lamentable. The vulnerability is troubling. A few families think it's extreme to try and meet routine costs—some need to plunge into their resources. As far as strength and holding power, the family and the business are extraordinary. Like this, they need to see conservations and cutbacks with the unfortunate moments.

The individuals who have lost their positions are, in this way, taking a gander at a significant stretch of

joblessness, cooped up for the most part inside their homes. Many would have managed their circumstance in protection without upsetting the family. What would we be able to do is comes a priority for all at this hour as educators too on importance. Start Small, Start some online business. Investigate some revenue of yours as a calling. Check the old recollections to be content. Have a go at cutting your costs and requests. Be together. Efficient attempt alternatives. They are searching for various acquiring choices regardless of whether they are more minor or excellent. Beware of conveying on the web range of instructing/preparing/ directing/the majority worldwide.

That is absolutely how I felt! As an educator. The teaching is on with no real students, in real-time physical classrooms. The learning is on but for sure at the independence of the learner. Likewise, preparation members and workshop crowds have been getting some information for quite a long time. So I chose to gather the ten best apparatuses and standards I know into a short, sharp course. Quite possibly, the most significant way to deal with flourishing in a VUCA world is the Pareto Principle, the 80:20 standard. The 80:20 principle says that you get 80% of the worth from the best 20% of the thoughts, and we end up applying it at the point when you use it skillfully. In this way, here is the best 20%. Apply it well, and you'll have an immense effect on your prosperity at work. Learning how to learn is the new priority.

The Uncertain Times!

"There are two things we can say with conviction about the future: it will be extraordinary. Like never before, pioneers need to explore new testing times, a reviving speed of progress, expanding assumptions, and a rising tide of quickly developing conditions. This unique and distinctive climate (VUCA) is moving pioneers to discover better approaches to lead their associations and make supported progress. Because of these conditions, there is a hunger for administration. Yet, pioneers face a tornado climate loaded with incredible freedoms and overwhelming difficulties to lead their kin and associations.

If I share the quote by Prof Sattar Bawany (2019), the Fourth Industrial Revolution (Industry 4.0) addresses a blend of Artificial Intelligence, Robotics, Cyber-Physical Systems and the Internet-of-Things (IoT). Authority 4.0 is about pioneers making their advanced change procedure and guaranteeing that it is lined up with their business and development plans. This is accomplished by showing successfully the set-up of next-generation initiative capabilities, which incorporate basic reasoning and imaginative speculation alongside enthusiastic and social knowledge abilities like sympathy and relationship with the board in particular.

Driving in the Fourth Industrial Revolution (Industry 4.0) spins around overseeing difficulties in a business climate that is profoundly problematic, progressively computerised and overwhelmingly unstable, unsure, mind-boggling and vague (VUCA). Innovative *headways in artificial brainpower, mechanical technology, sharing stages and the Internet of Things adjust action plans and businesses. These progressions are occurring at an uncommon speed. Pioneers at all levels need to foster the significant capabilities and abilities to effectively adapt to new fundamental factors when driving in a troublesome VUCA World.*

VUCA is an abbreviation that arose out of the military during the 1990s. It portrays the "haze of war" — the turbulent conditions experienced in an advanced combat zone. Its importance to pioneers in business is evident, as these conditions elucidate the climate where the company is led each day. Authority, not surprisingly, including making a dream, isn't sufficient in a VUCA world. TEACHING IN THE VUCA WORLD, a priority on cards, fetches the world of uncertainties. The new world order of VOLATILE, UNCERTAIN, COMPLEX, and AMBIGUOUS approaches reflect a new everyday learning and exploring the novel order of working.

• Volatile: Things change eccentrically, out of nowhere, very, particularly for the more regrettable.

• Uncertain: Important data isn't known or clear; suspicious, hazy about the current circumstance and future results; not ready to be depended upon.

• Complex: Many unique and associated parts: key choice factors, the connection between assorted

specialists, development, variation, coevolution, feeble signs.

· Ambiguous: Open to more than one translation; the significance of an occasion can be perceived unexpectedly.

Driving in a VUCA world not just gives a moving climate to pioneers to work and for chief advancement program to have an effect: it likewise gives an essential scope of new abilities. The new truth is acknowledging that new and various skills are required for pioneers to prevail in this new typical.

As educators, we need to guide our students and parents towards new destinations, which may include:

Flourish amid unpredictability, vulnerability, intricacy and equivocalness.

Recognise the need to choose what you centre around

Construct an essential organisation of essential contacts

Realise were to work at your pinnacle

Output your frame of reference for changes, patterns, dangers and openings

Bridle the basic achievement framework for life during the transition; the Powerhouse Loop

The Online Teaching and Learning with the Parents Support

Well, finally to explore the wonders amongst the PANDEMIC and the readiness to the VUCA world, without a doubt, the word VUCA causes some cocked eyebrows and characterizes the prepared idea of shock, an evoke stun, shock, or offense, ordinarily through whimsical activities or words. The expression regularly recommends negative consideration or judgment, however my dear companions, serves a reality today.

As a head of a school, I discover checking and testing easily of solace for the educators to be locked in and module to the learning situation. The range deceives our arrangement which screens thus, training has changed drastically, with the unmistakable ascent of e-learning, whereby educating is attempted distantly and on advanced stages. The paging is organized and characterized with the characteristic of conveying the classes without any difficulty and solace of their takers.

The target of this module enacts learning concerning the Leading Change in a Pandemic VUCA World specifically. The common vision and the methodology characterizes the destinations with introduction of understanding the idea in Visualizing the learning incredibly. It incorporates about the model to deal with the world through VOCA in the COVID period. Step by step instructions to prepare pioneers to oversee through. The idea represents the Volatility, Uncertainty, Complexity, Ambiguity, as VOCA practically speaking.

Without a doubt as training suppliers, our great work is to help everybody in giving quality schooling to all even in these extraordinary occasions. The reality lies that educators will in general do twofold and surprisingly threefold the task to convey. As we as a whole scramble to adapt to the quickly evolving COVID-19 circumstance, a significant number of us are unexpectedly taking on jobs as all day guardians and substitute educators likewise with the walk for the rush to convey.

The live streaming which the guardians requested sometime in the distant past mirror the ascent of new requests and wants. What is required is the need towards conveying the exercises to give every understudy customized criticism and work on, setting them up to benefit from study hall guidance.

Happy Learning to all on priority.

Ref:
    https://www.asmaindia.in/slc-2021/speaker/dr-dheeraj-mehrotra/

V

Quality Circles In Classrooms

QUALITY CIRCLES IN CLASSROOMS

Safety as a priority comes with unity. The circle activities go a long way in making learning visible in schools. The pride of learning counts with the conception of Learning with a unique index of education of heart and head in particular. The vital role of education being provided in schools deliver the pace of VALUE education as a parcelled knowledge base towards the masses. It is the education of the soul, believing in the pretext of "Learning to Learn" as a hobby rather than an occasional occurrence.

The holistic education as the word says talks about the overall education of head and heart with wisdom to deliver at pace. It is like knowing self with a belief of human values on priority with four pillars of learning, which includes, learning to learn, learning to know, learning to be and learning to work. The essence is to catch them young and innocent on priority. When we learn with pleasure we never forget. The choice is ours to deliver as teachers and educators to make the delivery and the deliberations in particular through the framework of pleasure and pride at the same time with the spiritual cult and the preface towards values and respect towards all religions of the world.

Wikipedia rightly defines, holistic education as: "Holistic education is a philosophy of education based on the premise that each person finds identity, meaning, and purpose in life through connections to the community, to the natural world, and to humanitarian values such as compassion and peace". Hence the unique blend of learning is through the meaningful attribute of knowing the purpose of life and self. The inclusion is about the self and the meaning of life into being alive and getting the purpose understood for the self and the objectives narrated towards excellence in particular. Respect for others towards recognition as support needs and connect with the nature, concerns towards the needy and the understanding of the universal brotherhood with implications towards peace and unity should be the concern over acceptance as a universal truth and virtue of life and living in totality.

Some of the necessities which integrate holistic education relate to the following:

Manners

Hands-on Lessons

Core Academics

Emotional Development

Critical Thinking Skills

Conflict Resolution Skills

Character Formation

Healthy Social Skills

Manners

One of the means to garner interest among the students to explore and inherit the essence of holistic attributes is through the inception of Quality circles in particular. Student Quality Circles' (SQC), is a means to develop group learning scenarios within schools. A Quality Circle is a group of people who come together and brainstorm over a common task and develop strategies towards Implementation.

In the field of academics, the concept of SQC has had its inception for over two decades and has taken its shape as one of the enriching tools towards excellence within classrooms.

A Student Quality Circle also known as SQC is a group of 5 to 15 student members, an ideal number is 8, who sit together in the form of a circle and discuss work-related problems. They accordingly evaluate the causes of the selected problem and try solving the same using the various quality tools and finally develop strategies to plan and execute the derivatives.

The encapsulation targets issues related to value system, universal brotherhood and knowing the beliefs and spectrum towards peace and harmony. In addition, the universal values are implemented through means of various interactive sessions in the schools which include the morning assemblies, PTM (Parent Teacher Meetings), Coffee Table with the Head of Schools during Class wise interactions and above all during the Annual Day functions. The initiative should be to imbibe in them the curiosity to learn *for life in particular. Some of the advantages which revolve around the holistic attributes within schools relate to the following:*

Improve Attention in Class

It is not a secret that many students find it hard to pay attention and concentrate in class. Surprisingly, laziness is not the real reason for this situation. In most cases, it is because stress, worries, fears and personal problems take their focus away from the lessons. This is where mindfulness meditation will play its role. Practising mindfulness can help the students to concentrate better because it directly influences the brain, especially the hippocampus part. And since it jogs the hippocampus to be more active, their memory and critical learning skill will be improved and help them get better grades.

Develop Better Interpersonal Skill

The competition and also pressure to always be the best in class can affect the student's social and emotional skills. They tend to only focus on themselves and don't care about what's happening around them. Interpersonal skill is very important to survive in the real world. So, the school must make sure that the pressure to perform well in school will not harm their interpersonal skill. Mindfulness training will also make the prefrontal cortex, the part of the brain that regulates emotion, more active. As a result, the students will be able to be more empathetic, more sociable as well as improve their behaviour in school.

Help Students Coping with Stress

It is very normal for students to experience stress when facing a challenging time in their education. However, the situation of the modern education system often forces the students to experience toxic stress, the kind of stress that can negatively affect their mental health. Stress is normal, but it can be dangerous when the students don't know how to deal with the stress. This is one of the main issues that mindfulness practice can solve. Mindfulness helps the students to see things more objectively and also relax their bodies and mind when facing a stressful situation.

School should not only focus on lessons and grades, but also education for life. The education system should really start to pay attention to the student's mental state too, and mindfulness meditation is one of the best methods for that. It will teach the students to be more mindful of the present, which can help them cope with stress, improve their optimism about life and also their performance in school. Schools do predict and practice innovative ways to deliver passion to the students. The yoga sessions and other mind-based exercises reveal an open spectrum of the level of mindfulness we need in our schools today.

Dr Dheeraj Mehrotra, Principal, Kunwar's Global School, Lucknow

VI
Guiding Students to be Independent Learners

Learning to learn as a priority has to have dwelled with the practice for a notion to live quality in academics. We as educators realise that Learning how to learn is a game-changer in the global knowledge spectrum, and it's never too early or, in fact, too late to teach students how to begin to learn more independently.

We stand to harness the roots of learning with innovation and creativity with the march of time. After a couple of years of remote and hybrid instruction, many students and teachers have become accomplished technology users and curators of knowledge, which has even resulted in leveraging sophisticated tech tools to facilitate learning both in and out of the classroom.

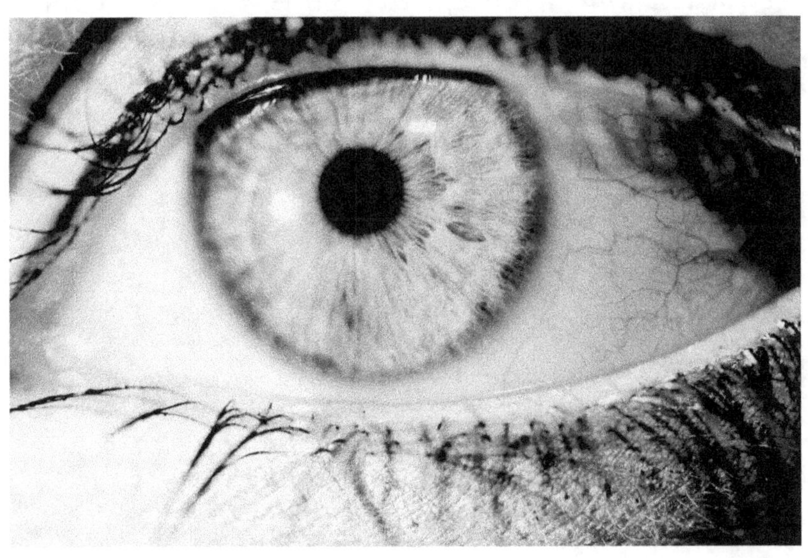

No more is the learning limited within the classrooms of the four walls, in particular. But like any area of expertise, there are always innovative ways to sharpen skills, streamline workloads, and increase access to and via technology in a big bang way!

The Priority

The same oration of the term "Independent learners" has a sense of meaning for self. It activates a module of learning by doing through engagement by interest and curiosity. This results in prioritising the sense of agency over their future. They have robust self-regulation and metacognitive skills and reflect their strengths and weaknesses deeply. The research reveals that Independent learners have an intellectual curiosity bolstered by an activated sense of extra-curricular activities, giving a novel dimension to SUPW in reality.

The priority hence appears to Encourage students to become self-disciplined learners. The teachers need to support them in committing themselves to achieving their goals. Assist them in affirming their commitment to organise themselves, manage their focus over time, and limit distractions. Help students learn to consistently define themselves as people who commit to and achieve their goals. It will probably be necessary to remind them that successful people forgive themselves when they make mistakes and then continue along the learning pathway. Pandemic or post-pandemic, the learning must continue.

Here comes the importance of being an independent learner who can take responsibility for their learning. These students can take the initiative and make good decisions without needing help from teachers. When students shift to independent learning, they often have more control over their time. This is to gaze their interest in learning through the concept of engagement and peer learning. The teachers are responsible for managing the spectrum via engagement and giving the activities related to employment and commitment via experiential learning.

The teachers should use the power of their relationship with students to show a passion for learning. When educators embody a passion for learning, their kids are more likely to be creative and engaging. They have a *powerful, positive emotional connection to education that will inspire their motivation to continue to learn. With teachers who release their passion for learning, students across all grades are free to learn new ways of learning with inspiration and joy. The fun element in the classroom not only engages the students but sure activates learning. The children, at times, are observed to be sleeping with their eyes open, otherwise. Over time, expect self-motivation rather than compliance.*

When students share stories about those who have inspired and impacted them, the whole classroom feels more connected. The apparent reason to Encourage students to tell a friend their learning goal and get their support has to be in practice and be the work in action. Action research is a big way when the students are given independence to learn independently. This is more challenging for the teachers and, above all, the parents who do not hence need to be worried about their kids. The development here is overall, all-around and inactivation.

This allows students to verbalise their goal, which will help them internalise it. Students of all ages are inherently social, and getting support from a peer can be very motivating. Giving students options for how they demonstrate their learning is an excellent way to ignite their curiosity.

The demand is for an Independent learner who takes responsibility for their learning by being self-motivated and accepting that frustration in the present is worthwhile to achieve future success. Teachers need to be curious and engage in what they're learning—Independent learners, to be so, ought to take the initiative. Encourage students to become self-disciplined learners. Please support them in committing themselves to getting started on achieving their goals. Assist them in affirming their commitment to organise themselves, manage their focus over time, and limit distractions.

authordheerajmehrotra.com   Rs. 200/- Only.

About the Author

Dheeraj Mehrotra has been honoured with the President of India's National Teacher Award in the year 2006 and the Best Science Teacher State Award, Innovation in Education for his inception of Six Sigma In Education by Education Watch, New Delhi and Education World- Best Teacher Award, BOLT Learner Teacher Award by Air India, 'Innovation in Education Award 2016' among others. He has developed over 150 FREE EDUCATIONAL MOBILE Apps for the Google Play Store exclusively for Teachers, Students, and Parents. This work has been recognised by the LIMCA BOOK OF RECORDS & INDIA BOOK OF RECORDS as the only Indian to draw that feast. Dr Mehrotra is presently working as a PRINCIPAL at KUNWARS GLOBAL SCHOOL, Lucknow, in India. He is an active TEDx speaker. As a premium UDEMY Instructor, he has also developed over 450 courses and is catering to over 8 Lakh students from 180 plus countries. He can be visited at www.authordheerajmehrotra.com